An Historical Account of the Life, Actions, and Conduct of Dr Archibald Cameron, Brother to Donald Cameron of Lochiel, Chief of That Clan Containing, I The Reasons Which Induced the Doctor to List Himself Among the Rebels

AN HISTORICAL

ACCOUNT

OF THE

LIFE, ACTIONS, and CONDUCT

OF

Dr. *Archibald Cameron,*

Brother to *Donald Cameron* of *Lo-chiel,* Chief of that Clan.

CONTAINING,

I. The Reasons which induced the Doctor to list himself among the Rebels.

II. His principal Business and Employment in the Chevalier's Army.

III. The Genealogy of the *Camerons,* traced up to their first Great Ancestor, with many curious Anec-dotes, relating to the Prowess and Magnanimity of several Chiefs of that Clan.

III. A Character and Description of the antient Highlanders, their Manners, Customs, Dress, Language, Hardiness, and peculiar Way of Life.

WITH

The Proceedings against him at the Court of *King's Bench,* his Behaviour at the *Tower* after Sentence, his taking Leave of his Wife and Friends, the Procession from the *Tower* to the Place of Execution, and his Behaviour there.

With a curious Print of Dr. CAMERON.

L O N D O N:

Printed for M. COOPER, in *Pater-noster-row,* W. REEVE, *Fleet-street,* and C. SYMPSON, at the *Bible-Warehouse, Chancery-lane.* 1753.

[Price Six-pence.]

AN HISTORICAL

ACCOUNT

OF THE

LIFE

OF

Dr. *ARCHIBALD CAMERON.*

N the Year 1745, now eight Years ago, *Charles Edward*, eldeſt Son of the Pretender, accompanied only with ſeven Perſons, landed in *Scotland.* The ſeven Companions of the young Adventurer were theſe following, *viz.* The Marquis of *Tullibardine*, eldeſt Brother to the Duke of *Athol,* who was attainted in 1713. 2. Old *Lochiel,* the Father of Dr. *Cameron,* who fought in the ſame Cauſe in 1715. 3. General *Macdonald,* a Lieutenant-general in the *Iriſh* Brigades. 4. Sir *Thomas Sherridan,* an *Iriſh* Gentleman, of a middle Age, and great Capacity. 5. Colonel *O Sullivan,* an *Iriſhman,* formerly a Prieſt, and Tutor to Marſhal *Maillebois's* Son. He was the young Chevalier's Director of the Artillery, and Aid de

A

Camp.

Camp. 6 Mr. *Kelly*, many Years a Prisoner in the Tower of *London*, on Account of the Affair of the Bishop of *Rochester* 7 Mr. *Michel*, many Years a Servant to the Old Chevalier, and, for the Affection he had to the Son, kept him Company in this Expedition

As soon as he was landed, he went to the House of *Donald Macdonald*, of *Kenloch Moidart*, from whence he sent out Letters to the adjacent Clans, to acquaint them with his Arrival. Upon which *Cameron* of *Lochiel*, after much Entreaty, went to him, and expressed his Surprize to see him so weakly attended, and positively refused to raise his Clan till the Chevalier could produce, in Writing, the *French* King's Resolution to assist him with a proper Number of Forces Being satisfied in this Point, he summoned his Clan, and set up his Standard, with this Motto, *Tandem triumphans*, *at length triumphant*. But at the same Time told him, That his Scheme was too ill concerted to expect Success from it, and that the Issue of it would be the Ruin of his Friends.

B u t, before we proceed farther, it may be proper to acquaint the Reader, that Dr *Cameron*, the Subject of our Memoirs, was in himself of a quiet and peaceable Temper, and had he not been Brother to the famous *Lochiel*, the warmest Stickler the Pretender had, it's very probable we should never have heard of him in this Rebellion

As his Father, *Evan Cameron*, of *Lochiel*, was the Chief of one of the most famous Clans in the Highlands, this his Son was educated in all the Branches of Learning which the best Schools or Universities of *Scotland* could afford. His Father designed him for the Bar; but young *Archibald* observing, that in order to be properly qualified for an Advocate, he must be Master of all the Quirks and sophistical Reasonings that are usually made Use of to puzzle a Cause, and hoodwink the Understanding with factitious Arguments. He therefore applied himself to the Study of a Science more agreeable to his natural Genius and Turn of Mind; and Physic was pitched upon, as what was more advantageous, and indeed more consonant to Mr. *Cameron*'s own Inclinations. In order to which, the Knowledge of the Human System was highly necessary For this Purpose, he applies himself to the Study of Anatomy, for without some tolerable Acquaintance with this, a Man will make but a very indifferent Figure either as a Physician or Surgeon. He therefore put himself under the Direction of Dr.
Alexander

Alexander Munro of the University of *Edinburgh*, a Gentleman of established Reputation, and justly esteemed for his extensive Knowledge in all the Branches of Surgery; which he has acquired not only by his own indefatigable Industry and judicious Observation, on the Variety of Cases that have come under his Cognizance, but has likewise improved his Judgment by attending to the Operations performed by his Father Dr *Munro*.

WHEN Mr *Cameron* had acquired a competent Skill in Anatomy, he applied himself to the Study of Physic, and herein was instructed by Dr *Sinclair*, a Gentleman very eminent in the Faculty. Having continued a convenient Time with Dr *Sinclair*, not content with the Progress he had already made, he resolves to Travel, and to improve himself in foreign Countries, in the Practice of an Art which he intended to make his Profession. Accordingly he went to *Paris*, where he had the best Opportunities of increasing his Knowledge. And being thus sufficiently qualified to exercise his Profession, he returned to *Lochabar*, where soon afterwards he married a young Lady of good Repute, whose Name was *Campbell*, who has made him the Father of seven Children, and is about seven Months gone with the eighth, unhappy for her and them, that they must be allotted so large a Share of Sufferings for his Crime, without being Partakers in his Guilt!

THUS Dr *Cameron*, who might have made a considerable Figure even in a Court, or a populous and well cultivated City, contents himself with exercising his Talents among a People, whose Manners and Fierceness resembled them very much to the wild Beasts of a Forest. Yet, by his gentle and humane Carriage among them, many were taught to follow a more honest Course of Life than is generally ascribed to the Highlanders, especially the *Camerons*, who have been reckoned the most infamous of all the Clans for their Thefts and Plunderings. The Doctor therefore took as much Pains in cultivating the Minds of these poor ignorant Wretches, as he did of their Bodies, in prescribing them proper Remedies in all their Illnesses. So that the whole Clan, by Means of his and his Brother's Instructions and Regulations, were greatly reformed in their Morals; Honesty and Industry increased every-where by the Encouragement given by their Patrons, who took all imaginable Pains to instruct them in the Principles of Justice and Reli-

gion

gion, and to civilize their Manners by teaching them to behave like rational and ſociable Creatures.

As the Highlanders in all Reigns have been remarkable for diſturbing the eſtabliſhed Government of *Scotland*, by taking up Arms on every Invaſion for the Invaders, and have been the Ringleaders and chief Promoters of the Rebellion, which, on this Occaſion, had almoſt ruined that Kingdom, I believe it will not be amiſs to give a Character of them from Hiſtory.

Buchanan, the *Scots* Hiſtorian, ſays, They are as parſimonious as the Antients in their Diet, Appaiel, and Furniture. They fiſh and hunt for their Food, and while they hunt, eat it raw, after having ſqueezed out the Blood. Their Drink is Meat-broth, or Whey, of which they have Plenty at their Entertainments, but moſt of them drink Water. Their Bread is a very artiul Compoſition of Oats and Bailey, the only Grain which their Country produces. After eating a little of it in the Morning, they hunt, or go about their Buſineſs, without eating any more till Night. They delight moſt in Cloaths of ſeveral Colours, eſpecially ſtriped, and the Colours they are fondeſt of aie Purple and Blue. Their Anceſtors, as many of them do ſtill, made uſe of Plaids very much variegated, but now they make them rather of dark Colours, more like the Crops of Heath, that they may not be diſcovered while they lie in Heaths waiting for Game. Being rather wrapped up than covered with their Plaids, they endure all the Rigouis of the Seaſons, and ſometimes ſleep covered all over with Snow. At home they lie upon the Ground, having under them Fern or Heath (covered with a Sheet or Blanket) the latter laid with the Roots undermoſt, ſo that it is almoſt as ſoft as Feathers, and much more healthful, for the Quality of Heath being to draw out ſuperfluous Humours, when they lay down weary and faint upon it at Night, they riſe fieſh and vigorous in the Morning. They affect this haid way of Sleeping, and whenever they happen to come into Places where there is better Accommodation, they pull the Coverings off the Bed, and lie down upon them wrapped in their Plaids, leſt they ſhould be ſpoiled by what they call ſuch a *barbarous Effeminacy*.

The old *Scots* Language, call'd *Erſe*, has loſt ſo much Ground by the Spreading of the *Engliſh* in *Scotland*, ever
ſince

fince the *Norman* Conqueſt, that 'tis now confined to the Highlands, and the Iſles, where moſt of the People of Note do alſo underſtand an I ſpeak *Engliſh*.

Mr *Mackay* tells us, that the Highlanders differ as much from the Lowlanders in their Dreſs, Manners, and Language, as the *Indians* of *Mexico* do from the *Spaniards*; that the old *Scots* Language is here ſpoken in its native Purity, and written in its genuine Characters, which are more like the *Greek* or *Hebrew* than the *Roman*; whereas the *Welſh*, tho' they have preferved their Language, yet have intirely loſt their old Character, and write in the *Roman*.

'Tis preſumed that we cannot have a better Authority for what remains to be ſaid of the Nature of the Highlanders, whom *Tacitus* calls *Horeſti*, i. e. *Montani*, or *Mountaineers*, than the Account which is given of them by that eminent Antiquary, Sir *James Dalrimple*, Uncle to the late Earl of *Stair*, in his *Obſervations on* Cambden's *Britain*, and this we ſhall give our Readers in his own Words, *viz*

' The Inhabitants of theſe Regions, are a Kind of
' rude, warlike, quarrelſome, and miſchievous People;
' who being the unmix'd Progeny of the antient *Scots*,
' ſpeak *Iriſh*, and call themſelves *Albannik* The i Bodies
' are firmly and compactly made, withal ſtrong and
' nimble of Foot, high-minded, bred in warlike Exer-
' ciſes, and inured to Robberies on their Neighbours; and
' upon a Hatred, moſt deſperately forward to take Re-
' venge. They lived by Hunting, Fiſhing, Fowling, and
' Stealing, and, like the *Spaniards*, wear long Hair.
' They are divided into Kindreds and Families, which
' they call *Clans*, and are ſo united to the Cauſe of their
' particular Clans, that there is an Act of Parliament,
' that if any one of a Clan does a Miſchief, the whole Clan
' is anſwerable for it, and they muſt either deliver up the
' Aggreſſor, or the firſt Man that is apprehended ſuffers
' for it, and the whole Clan bears Feud for the Hurt
' received by any one Member of it, even altho' they
' ſuffer juſtly. Many Gentlemen in the Highlands ſhun
' one another's Company, leſt they ſhou'd revive a Quar-
' rel that happen'd between their Fore-fathers, perhaps
' three hundred Years ago. They are always warm in
' their Friendſhips, for if they meet with one in Amity
' with

' with their own Clan, be it in any Country of the
' World, there is immediately the most intimate Friend-
' ship The *Macdonalds* are by much the most powerful
' of all the Clans They are divided into four Classes, and
' inhabit distinct Countries. The *Macdonalds* of *Glengary*
' dwell upon the *Lockness*, the *Macdonalds* of *Slate*, in
' *Lacheber* and the Isle of *Skey*, the Captain of *Clan-Ro-*
' *nald*, and *Macdonald* of *Keppoch*, and those of *Kintyre*,
' towards *Argyleshire*. The other Clans, *Clan-Katin*,
' *Clan-Cameron*, the *Macleans*, and almost innumerable
' other *Macs*, altho' independent of one another, yet are
' entirely guided by the *Macdonalds*, who have been so
' powerful, as often to assume the Name of *Kings of the*
' *Isles*; and one of them in 1461, according to Mr Ry-
' mer's *Fœdera*, enter'd into a League with *Edward* IV.
' of *England*. *Robert*, the first of the *Stuart* Kings of
' *Scotland*, married his Daughter *Margaret* to *Macdonald*,
' Lord of the Isle, to serve him in his Interest; but all
' would not do; they were the common Disturbers of the
' Nation, till *James* V. privately with a Body of Men,
' took Shipping, and landed in every Clan and Island, and
' brought them in Person to his Obedience, making them
' give Hostages for their good Behaviour.'

BESIDES the Methods taken, as we have already men-
tion'd, for reducing and reforming the Highlanders, 'tis
proper just to take Notice of two or three Acts passed in
the Reign of K. *George* I. which contributed, not a little,
to that End.

[I] 1 *George*, Cap. 20. An Act for encouraging all
Superiors, Vassals, Landlords and Tenants, who continue
loyal to King *George*.

[II] 1 *George*, Cap. 54. An Act enjoining, That the
personal Service and Attendance, which was wont to be
the Heads of Clans, and Owners of Estates, at the Plea-
sure of such Chiefs, under the Names of personal Attendance, Hosting, Hunting, Watching, and Warding,
shall be for the future paid in Money annually, and the
said personal Service, &c shall be utterly annulled This
Act was farther enforced in the 11th of the same Reign,
Cap 26. on the Non-observance of the former by many of
the contemptuous Highlanders.

[III] 1 *George*, Cap. 54. An Act for more effectual
securing the Highlands of *Scotland*, which enacted, 'That
no Person within the said Highlands, shall use or bear
Broad-

Broad-fwords or Target, Ponyard, Wingar, or Durk, Side-piftol or Gun, or any warlike Weapon in the Fields, or in the Way to or from any Church, Market, Fair, Burial, Huntings, Meetings, &c. However, not to extend to Noblemen, Officers of Juftices, or Commanders, having yearly 400 *l. Scots*, or who are otherwife qualified to vote at Elections for Parliament, allowing to every fuch Commander two Firelocks, two Pair of Piftols, and two Swords; and that the Magiftrates of the Royal Burghs may keep Arms in Magazines.

THIS, I believe, is a very juft Defcription of the Highlanders, that is, fuch as they were at and before the Time of the late Rebellion; but were then fo entirely broken and fubdued, that the Government has found but little Difficulty in taming their rough and favage Tempers, and in making them good and ufeful Subjects.

THE Clan *Cameron*, of which *Lochiel* was the Chief, was one of the moft numerous and brave that then inhabited the Highlands of *Scotland*, but being ftrongly attached to the *Stuart* Intereft, have always appeared for the Pretender upon any Invafion, or Commotions raifed in that Kingdom in Favour of his Caufe, and in the late Rebellion none of the Clans behaved more ftrenuoufly, even to the laft, for the young Chevalier, than the *Camerons*, who, with *Lochiel* their Chief at their Head, were the firft in all the Battles and Skirmifhes fought with the King's Troops, and were the laft that retired out of the Field. Even after the Battle of *Culloden*, when the young Pretender's Affairs were fo defperate, that there was no Profpect or vifible Means of retrieving them, when all the Clans were entirely broke and difperfed, and a great part of them cut off and deftroyed, the *Camerons* did not forfake him, but did all in their Power to put a better Face on his Affairs, protected him when purfued by his Enemies, and for a long while fecreted him in inacceffible Places in the Mountains.

As Dr. *Cameron* was a Man of no Ambition, but of a quiet and eafy Temper, the Reader muft not expect to find him engaged in any notable Exploits; his only or chief Bufinefs in the Army being to attend his Brother *Lochiel*, and to affift him with his Skill if any Difafter fhould happen to befal him in Battle. In order therefore to diverfify our Story, which would be very fhort were it confined wholly to the Doctor, I have collected, from a little Tract publifhed foon after the Rebellion, fome diverting Anecdotes

dotes relating to this famous Family from which he is descended.

THE Family of *Camerons*, says my Author, is certainly very antient, and pretend a Settlement in that Country long before the *Irish* had any Possessions there, and disclaim all Manner of Relation to them. *Lochiel*, their late Chief, boasted, that some of his Ancestors were settled there above seven hundred Years ago But I presume he could bring no Proof of this more than Tradition, since the Division of Lands, and Settlement of Property by Writings (which were the only Methods of tracing the Antiquity of Families) did not commence till some Hundreds of Years after that Period. No Records nor Registers, nor Genealogies so antient, can at this Day be produced, nor was there any Sort of Learning cultivated among them, in those Times, but what was found among the *Druids* and Poets, who were retained by Persons of Figure to commemorate, in Verses and Songs, the mighty Deeds of their Ancestors; by which Means a sort of traditionary Genealogy was handed from Father to Son. But other Vouchers they had none, till a Division of Property was settled by Writings, in which the Names of the Possessors must necessarily be introduced, and so continued down in Order to Posterity

THESE Bards or poetical Genealogists, we may be sure, never run the Hazard of their Patron's Favour, by rehearsing such Deeds or Actions which might make a Blot in their Escutcheons, nothing which might seem to lessen the lineal and inherent Virtues of the Family must be introduced. Their Business was to sing Encomiums to their Heroes, and magnify and extol the great Atchievements of those Worthies from whom their Patrons claimed their Descent; and therefore it is no Wonder if we find but little Truth, or have the greatest Reason to suspect the Veracity of such of their Genealogies as are carried higher than the Time when Learning came more generally into Repute, and the History of private Persons as well as public Transactions, might be transmitted to Posterity by the Means of Printing.

THERE is not a Family among the Clans, but whose Ancestors were most of them Heroes, or Persons who had arrived to the Tip-top of military Glory, at least their Bards have represented them so, but none they have bedecked so egregiously as the Family of the *Camerons*, which they have so inveloped in Fable, that scarce
                                                                    the

the Glimmerings of Probability appear thro' the greatest Part of the Story. It will therefore be to little Purpose to trace the Genealogy of his Family any higher than the first of the Name, who settled upon the Estate of *Lochiel*.

The first Man who was called by the Name of *Cameron*, was much renowned for his Feats in Arms, and his prodigious Strength; a Monument of which is still remaining near *Aclnacary*, the Seat of *Lochiel*, namely, a large Stone, of upwards of 500 Weight, which he could hoist from the Ground with a strait Arm, and toss it with as much Ease, as a Man does a Cricket-ball, a Plough-share he could bend round his Leg like a Garter; and the strongest Ropes were no more in his Hands than Twine-thread. In short, he seems to have been a second *Sampson*, with this Difference only, that our *Cameron* seems not to have been so easily inveigled by the Women as the *Jew* was, nor did his Strength lie in his Hair.

This Man of Might was so conscious of his Strength and Prowess, that he thought no Man upon Earth was a Match for him, and accordingly entered the Lists with the most famous Champions of that Age, nor was afraid to challenge the most renowned of them. In one of their Combats, it seems, his Antagonist handled him very roughly, and with a violent Blow of his Fist set his Nose awry, for the Encounter was accidental, and consequently both unarmed, for had they fought with Swords, he might have hew'd it quite off, but this blunt Blow only set it on one Side, yet so, as that it could never be recovered to its right Position. From this Accident he was always afterwards called *Cameron*, or, *The Knight of the wry Nose*, as that Word imports in the *Highland* Language.

Our Hero was now arrived at the 35th Year of his Age, and had given many signal Proofs of his Valour, so that his Name became terrible all over the Country. But having little or no paternal Estate, he began to think it highly necessary for him to join himself to some great and powerful Family, the better to enable him to distinguish himself more eminently, than it was possible for him to do as a single Man, without Friends or Relations, or at least such as were of little or no Account. He had spent his Life in the Shire of *Dumbarton*, but as he had no Family or Inheritance to incumber him, he resolved

C   to

to try his Fortune in the World, and to go in Search of
a Wife   He set out accordingly, and happened to light
on that Part of the Country where *Lochiel's* Estate now
lie   Here he informed himself of the Character and
Circumstances of the Chief who resided there, and un-
derstood that he was a Man of a large Estate, had a
great Number of Friends and Dependants, and withal
had a fair and excellent young Lady to his Daughter   This
was a Foundation sufficient for our wry-nose Knight to
build his Hopes and future Expectations upon   He soon
made himself known to the Gentleman, whose Name
was *M'Tavish*, Baron of *Straborgig*, to whom having
given an Account of himself and his Business (for his
Fame was there before) he was kindly welcomed, and
treated with all the Civilities imaginable.   In short, a
Bargain was soon struck for the Daughter, who was as
well pleased as the Father, with the Offer of a Husband
so much to her Liking, for Strength of Body, vigorous
and sinewy Limbs, and undaunted Courage, were, in
those Days, the best Qualifications to recommend a Man
to the Affections of a Lady.

· The Baron of *Straborgig* was the more willing to
marry his Daughter to our Knight, because by this Al-
liance he should get a brave bold Man to head his People
against the Clan of *M'Donalds* of *Glengary*, who border-
ing on the *Lochiel's* Estate, there were frequent Bickerings
and Skirmishes between the two Clans; for in those Days
all Quarrels and Disputes were decided by the Strength of
the Arm, and the Edge of the Sword   Our Knight,
whose Courage never flinch'd in the greatest Dangers, led
on his Men boldly, and fought many bloody Encounters
with the *M'Donalds*, whose Chief he challenged to single
Combat; but *M'Donald* knowing his Antagonist was su-
perior to him in Strength, refused, but fought it out with
him in a pitched Battle, in which however he was worsted,
and great Numbers of his People slain, and finding himself much weakened, and his Clan greatly diminished
since the Knight of the Wry-nose became his Enemy, he
proposed a Compromise between the two Families, which
was agreed to, and the Chiefs on both Sides met (each
attended with a numerous Retinue, to prevent Surprize)
in a certain Meadow that lay, as it were, between both
Estates, and which both laid a Claim to.   Here the Mat-
ters in Difference were solemnly and amicably debated;
and

and at length the Parties came to this Conclusion That *McDonald* should, for him and his Heirs, for ever renounce all his Claim and Pretence of Right to such a certain District, containing about 500 Acres of Land, with all the Royalties, Privileges, and Prerogatives thereunto belonging and appertaining, the contending for which had occasioned innumerable Feuds and Quarrels, and the Effusion of a great deal of innocent Blood, this he solemnly assigned and made over to the Knight of the Wry-nose, and his Heirs for ever.

This is the Story which the *Highland* Bards have recorded of this great Progenitor of the *Camerons*, and these are the Means, they tell us, by which he got Possession of an Estate worth about 100 *l* a Year. The Registers of this Family record likewise a long Succession of great Men, who rendered themselves famous by their military Exploits, but the Genealogy is so wrapped up in Fable and Romance, that a Relation of them would appear much in the same Light, as the Histories of St. *George*, St. *Dennis*, *Guy* Earl of *Warwick*, *John of Gaunt*, nd other fabulous Heroes, wrote for the Diversion and Amusement of Children. Let it suffice to assure the Reader, that there has been a lineal Succession of great Men in this Family, and that the Chief of the House, for the time being, had always distinguish'd himself by some remarkable Actions and Atchievements, and had added either Glory or Enlargement to his Clan, down from the Knight of the Wry-nose to *Lochiel* their late Representative, the Brother of Dr. *Cameron*, the Subject of these Memoirs. It appears plainly enough, that they were always a powerful Clan, because they have been so far from losing or diminishing any Part of their Estate, that they have made great Additions to it in the Course of several Ages. Their Chiefs were likewise always careful to strengthen their Interest with potent and honourable Alliances, by marrying their Children into the best Families in the Shires of *Argyle* and *Invernefs*; and their Estate, which is reckoned at about 500 *l per Ann* is held in Vassalage, partly of the Duke of *Gordon*, and partly of the Duke of *Argyle*.

We come now to the more immediate Ancestors of this Family, and we shall go no farther back than Sir *Hugh Cameron*, Grandfather of the late *Lochiel* and his Brother the Doctor, who was a strenuous Partizan for

King,

King *Charles* I It is reported of him, that one Day, he a d his Party being engag'd with a Detachment from *Cromwell's* Army, he was thrown down by one of the *English* Soldiers, and disarmed, but though Sir *Hugh* was at the Mercy of the Soldier, who might have taken his Life, but offer'd him Quarter, yet so strong was his Antipathy to the very Name of an *Englishman*, that he scorn'd to accept it, and suddenly jumping up, seiz'd with his Teeth fast hold of the Soldier's Throat, which he could not be forced from, 'till he had tore a Hole in the Fellow's Windpipe, and so kill'd him on the Spot.

Evan Cameron, his Son, imbib'd the same Aversion to the *English*, and carried it to as great Lengths in every Instance of his Life, or as often as Opportunity serv'd him to shew it, and he had so inseparably attach'd himself to the Family of the *Stuarts*, that no Consideration whatever could induce him to abandon that Party, or forsake their Interests At the Revolution, no Man was a more zealous Asserter of the Rights of K *James* than he, and was actually in Arms, and serv'd the Lord *Dundee*, who being defeated, *Evan* thought it highly necessary for him to leave his own Country, and retire to *France*, and resided for many Years at the Court of St. *Germains*, subsisting on a Pension allow'd him by the *French* King, and when, by the Treaty of *Utrecht*, the Pretender was obliged to quit *France*, *Evan* follow'd him to *Avignon*, and was with him afterwards at *Rome*, though not always, as some of that Faction have been, but made his chief Residence at *Paris* In the Year 1715, he came over to *Scotland* with the Pretender, but I can recollect nothing memorable of him in that Expedition, and he went back again with his Master to *France*.

When the late Rebellion broke out in 1745, he embark'd with the Chevalier in the Expedition to *Scotland*, where, though he was eighty Years of Age, he behaved with surprizing Activity, and bore all the Fatigues of that rough Campaign with uncommon Fortitude and Steadiness, and sat and managed his Horse with a Gracefulness and Agility, scarce paralell'd by any Officer in the Rebel Army, however he lost his Life at the Battle of *Culloden*, in Defence of his pretended Prince; and 'twas Pity his Courage and other good Qualities had not been employ'd in a better Cause.

During

During the old Gentleman's Refidence at *Paris*, only his youngeft Son the Doctor went to fee him, and that not purpofely, but as it were cafually For the Doctor's Defign in going to *Paris*, was, as before intimated, to improve himfelf in the Knowledge of Phyfick, and not to fettle a Correfpondence or concert Meafures with the dif-affected Party, in order to advance the Pretender's In-tereft The Bent of his Genius led him to the Study of the Sciences, and the pacifick Temper of his Mind with-held him from engaging in the dangerous Enterprizes of Politicks And therefore in vifiting his Father, he had no other View than to pay him that filial Duty which became him, without any Defign of learning any of his political Principles

As to *Lochiel*, the elder Son, he never was Abroad with his Father, but lived quietly at Home upon his Eftate ; he had not imbibed thofe inveterate Principles againft the *Englifh* and the Royal Family, as his Predeceffors had done, and never fhewed any Inclination to difturb the Govern-ment for the Sake of a foreign Intereft, and, all Circum-ftances confidered and compared, we are pretty fure, that he knew nothing of the intended Invafion, till the young Pretender was actually landed in *Scotland* For upon a Mufter of his whole Clan, they had not a hundred Stands of Arms among them all, and but few of them in a Condition for Ufe, nor had he any Provifion to furnifh them with better. 'Tis true, when the Chevalier was actually landed, his Father fent him exprefs Orders to raife the whole Clan immediately, and come with them to join the Pretender *Lochiel* however was far from being ready to obey his Summons, he was fenfible of the Rifque he run, not only in his Perfon, but his Eftate, he con-fider'd, that at prefent he lived very happily, unmolefted and unenvied by any Body ; but fhould he comply with his Father's Requeft, and the Enterprize fhould mif-carry, he fhould be utterly ruined without a Poffibility of Redemption. Thefe Reafons were ftrong and cogent, and kept him a good while irrefolute, or rather firm to his Purpofe of not meddling in fo dangerous an Affair, and fo continued, notwithftanding all the Solicitations made to him to change his Mind, for the Space of fix Weeks, the Chevalier and his Father were all that Time at the Houfe of *Mc Donald* of *Kinloch Moidart* At laft the young Pretender himfelf came to his Houfe at *Achna-*

carry,

cary, with about fifty Perfons in his Retinue, together with old *Cameron* his Father. On their Arrival, the old Gentleman fhew'd himfelf immediately to his Clan, who were greatly rejoiced to fee their old Chief among them again; fo that it was now next to impoffible for young *Lochiel* to make any longer Refiftance, and in fine, he joined in their Meafures, and he and his Father had the Command given them of the Clan, who were directly convocated and arm'd.

At the breaking out of the Rebellion, the Clan of the *Camerons* were judg'd to confift of about 800 fighting Men, fit to bear Aims, bold, ftout Fellows, and train'd up in the Exercife of Arms But what was more to their Praife, they were not fo addicted to pilfering and robbing their Neighbours, which moft of the other Clans in the *Highlands* were notorious for, particularly the *McDonalds* For young *Lochiel* being a Man of Honour and Probity himfelf, took abundance of Pains, nor was his Brother the Doctor lefs affiduous in reforming the People of his Clan, and to infufe into them true Notions of Juftice and Honefty And as *Lochiel* was the chief Magiftrate amongft them, he punifh'd their Exceffes with a becoming Seve-rity, and at the fame Time endeavour'd to inculcate into them better Principles, and jufter Notions of Right and Wrong than they had hitherto learnt. So that though he was both beloved and feared by great Numbers of them, yet there were many who hated both him and his Bro-ther, becaufe they would not fuffer them to fpoil and plunder their Neighbours, which was allow'd by moft of the other Chiefs of the Clans, but *Lochiel* little regarded their Clamour on that Account, he knew his Authority was fufficient to keep them in Subjection, and he gave himfelf no Trouble about any Thing they fhould report againft his Adminiftration What Pity it is that two Gentlemen of fo much Worth, and who might have done excellent Service to their King and Country, fhould be over-aw'd by their Father to rebel againft both, and that too againft their own Principles, and jufter Way of Thinking.

But tho' *Lochiel* was at length prevailed upon to fet up the Chevalier's Standard, yet his Brother, the Doctor, could not for a good while be prevailed with to join in their Meafures, nay, it was chiefly owing to his Remon-ftrances, that *Lochiel* fo long withftood the earneft and

conftant

onftant Solicitations of his Father and the Chevalier. But when *Lochiel* had once lifted himfelf in his Service, his Honour was fo deeply engaged, that no Arguments or Perfuafions could prevail with him to defift. But when he had muftered his Clan, and fet up his Standard, he found that his Brother had left him in Difguft. This gave him a good deal of Difquietude; for he could not bear the Thought, that one fo nearly related to him, fhould have a feparate Intereft. Upon which he fent a Meffenger to him with an Order, requiring his immediate Attendance. The Doctor obeyed, but could not fo eafily be wrought upon to concur in his Brother's new Schemes. He remonftrated, in the ftrongeft Terms, upon the unfurmountable Obftacles that he forefaw would attend the Undertaking, and the terrible Confequences of a Mifcarriage. *Lochiel*, however, would take no Denial, telling him, that he did not want the Affiftance of his Sword, or his Valour, but only defired he would attend him as his Companion, that he might always have the Advantage of his Advice and Skill, in cafe the Fortune of War fhould render either of them neceffary. The Doctor, how ill foever he thought of the Caufe, yet his Affection for his Brother, and the many fignal Obligations he lay under to him, at length prevailed over all other Confiderations, and he fubmitted to fhare his Brother's Fate, whatever it fhould be.

But tho' the Doctor was, with great Reluctance, and in a Manner forced to join his Brother's Meafures, yet he abfolutely refufed to accept of any Commiffion in the Army, neither did he act there, as ever I could learn, in any other Quality than as a Phyfician. He was perfectly unacquainted with the military Art, and therefore wholly unqualified to give his Advice, or even his Vote in Council, upon any Operations that were propos'd by the Chiefs or general Officers. Yet, as he was always among them, it is fuppos'd, at leaft in the Eye of the Law, that he countenanced, encourig'd, and, as much as it was in his Power, affifted the Rebels, in all their Outrages againft the Government.

Dr *Cameron* was of fo humane a Difpofition, that if Credit may be given to general Report, when any wounded Prifoners were brought to him, he was as affiduous in his Care of them, as if they had fought in the Caufe he efpoufed, and 'tis affirmed, that he never refus'd his

Affiftance

Affiftance to any one that afk'd it, whether Friend or Foe.

The Chevalier having increas'd his Army to about 2000, march'd forward, in order to enter upon Action, and advanced to *Corryerroig*, a Hill about fix Miles from Fort *Auguftus*, and being inform'd that General *Cope* was coming to attack him, waited for him with a Refolution to hazard a Battle, if the Enemy was in the fame Humour. The General, however, either diftrufting his own Strength, or for fome other Reafon, beft known to himfelf, march'd forward to *Aberdeen*, where he embark'd his Army on Board fome Ships, which tranfported it to *Dunbar*, the neareft and beft Place for landing on the South Side of the *Firth*, and there difembark'd.

The Chevalier, perceiving the Enemy had left him, put his Army in Motion, and directed his March to *Perth*, of which he took Poffeffion, where his Father was proclaim'd King, and himfelf Regent of *Scotland*. Here he was join'd by feveral more of the Clans. After fome Stay, he decamp'd from *Perth*, and proceeded in his March, till he approach'd *Edinburgh*, of which City he foon got Poffeffion. But by what Means, and of his Behaviour there, and afterwards, we muft refer the Reader to the Annals of that Time, it not being our Defign to write a Hiftory of the Rebellion, but only to relate fuch Paffages and Tranfactions of it, wherein *Lochiel* or his Brother had fome Concern.

The Chevalier having, with very little Trouble, got Poffeffion of *Edinburgh*, it was not long before he was inform'd, that General *Cope* was on the March to attack him. Upon which News he led out his Army to meet and fight him. Accordingly Battle was joined at a Place called *Prefton-Pans*, which proved fatal to the Royalifts. Juft as the Army was marching to the Attack, the Chevalier appeared at their Head, very alert, and ready to lead them to the Onfet. *Lochiel*, however, who had a very great Refpect and Efteem for him, earneftly entreated him to forbear expofing his Perfon, and advifed him to take his Stand upon a rifing Ground, under the Guard of a Party, from whence he might fend his Orders to any Part of the Army during the Engagement, as he fhould fee Occafion; for if any Misfortune fhould befal him, they were all ruined to a Man, and that too much depended on his Safety, to hazard his Perfon without more
apparent

apparent Neceffity than there was, which Advice the Chevalier follow'd, and retired with a Party to a high Field to the South-weft of *Seatoun*.

The Chevalier, after the Advantage gain'd at *Prefton-pans*, march'd his Army into *England*, but as during that whole Expedition, fcarce any remarkable Action happen'd, befides plundering defencelefs Towns, *Lochiel* had no Opportunity to diftinguifh himfelf, till his Return into *Scotland*. At the Battle of *Falkirk*, he, at the Head of his *Camerons*, vigoroufly attack'd the King's Troops, and very much contributed to turn the Fortune of the Day, but in the Heat of the Action, was wounded by a Mufket-ball in his Leg; which being obferv'd by his Brother the Doctor, who always kept near his Perfon, he begg'd him to retire to have it drefs'd; which he accordingly did, but as the Doctor was lending him his Affiftance, he himfelf receiv'd a flight Wound.

On the Duke of *Cumberland*'s Arrival in *Scotland*, the Chevalier retired further North, and took up his Head Quarters at *Invernefs*; from whence he fent out Parties to fkirmifh with the Royalifts; and many Encounters happen'd between them with various Succefs. During thefe Hoftilities, an Opportunity fell out, which gave *Lochiel* an Occafion to difcover the Generofity of his Sentiments, and his Abhorrence to Cruelties of all Kinds. Thus it was.

The *Campbels* having, all along, exerted themfelves very ftrenuoufly in Behalf of the Government, had thereby exceedingly exafperated the Rebels, but efpecially *Cameron* of *Lochiel*, and *Alexander Macdonald* of *Keppoch*. Thefe two Gentlemen wrote the following Letter to Mr. *Stewart* of *Invernakel*, dated *Glenturs, March* 20. 1746.

Sir,

YESTERNIGHT we receiv'd a Letter from *Clunie*, giving an Account of the Succefs of the Party fent by his R---- H---- (the *Chevalier*) under the Command of the Lord *George Murray*, to *Athol*; a Copy of which Letter we thought proper to fend you inclofed; as you happen, for the prefent, to lie contiguous to the *Campbels*, 'tis our fpecial Defire, that you inftantly communicate to *Airds* the Sheriff, and other leading Men among them, our Sentiments, (which God willing, we are determined to execute) by tranfmitting this our Letter, and the inclofed Copy, to any the neareft to you.

D

It

IT is our Opinion, that, of all Men in *Scotland*, the
Campels had the leaft Reafon of any, to engage in the
prefent War againft his R---- H-----'s Intereft, confidering they have always appear'd in Oppofition to the R-----
Family fince the Reign of *James* VI. and have been guilty
of fo many Acts of Rebellion and Barbarity during that
Time, that no injur'd Prince but would endeavour to re-
fent it, when God was ever pleafed to put the Power in
his Hands. Yet his prefent M----y, and his R--- H------
the Prince Regent, were gracioufly pleafed, by their re-
fpective Declarations, to forgive all paft Mifcarriages to the
moft virulent and inveterate Enemy, and even bury them
in Oblivion, provided they returned to their Allegiance;
and tho' they fhould not appear perfonally in Arms, in
Support of their P------'s Caufe, yet their ftanding Neuter
would entitle them to the good Graces of their injur'd
Sovereign. But in Spight of all the Lenity and Clemency,
that a Prince could fhew or promife, the *Campbels* have
openly appear'd, with their wonted Zeal for Rebellion and
Ufurpation, in a moft officious Manner, nor could we
ever form a Thought to ourfelves, that any Men, endow'd
with Reafon and common Senfe, would ufe their Fellow-
Cieatures with that Inhumanity and Barbarity, as they do;
and of which we have daily Proofs by their burning of
Houfes, ftripping of Women and Children, expofing them
to the open Fields, and the Severity of the Weather, burning of Corn, houghing (*ham-ftringing*) of Cattle, and
killing of Horfes To enumerate the Whole, would
be too tedious at this Time. They muft naturally re-
flect that we cannot but look upon fuch Cruelties with
Horror and Deteftation, and, with Hearts full of Revenge,
will certainly endeavour to make Reprifals; and we are determined to apply to his R---- H----- for Leave and an
Order to enter their Country, with full Power to act at
Difcretion; and if we are lucky enough to obtain it, we
fhall fhew, that we are not to make War againft Women,
and the Biute Creation, but againft Men, and as God
was pleafed to put fo many of them in our Hands, we
hope to prevail with his R---- H----- to hang a *Campbel*
for every Houfe that fhall hereafter be burnt by them.

NOTWITHSTANDING the many fcandalous and ma-
licious Afperfions, induftroufly contrived by our Enemies,
they could never, fince the Commencement of the War,
impeach us with any Acts of Hoftility, that had the leaft
Tendency

Tendency to fuch a Cruelty, tho' we had it in our Power, if barbarous enough to execute it.

When Courage fails againſt Men, it betrays Cowardiſe to a great Degree, to vent the Spleen againſt Brutes, Houſes, Women, and Children, that cannot refiſt We are not ignorant of their villainous Intentions, by the intercepted Letter from the Sheriff *Airds*, &c. which plainly diſcovers, that it was by their Application, that their General *Cumberland* granted Orders for burning, &c. which he could not be anſwerable for to the *Britiſh* Parliament, being moſt certain, that ſuch Barbarity could never be countenanced by any Chriſtian Senete,

(*Sign'd*)   Donald Cameron, of *Lachiel*.
        Alex. Mac Donnell of *Keppoch*.

I Cannot omit taking Notice, that my People have been the firſt that have felt the cowardly Barbarity of my pretended *Campbel* Friends ; I ſhall deſire to live, to have an Opportunity of thanking them for it in the open Field.
(*Sign'd*)   Donald Cameron.

The Battle of *Culloden*, which put a final Period to the Rebellion, and all the Pretender's Hopes of ſitting on the *Britiſh* Throne, was likewiſe fatal to vaſt Numbers of his Followers and Adherents, Multitudes of whoſe Carcaſes ſpread the bloody Field , and they that eſcaped, were but reſerved to ſuffer infinite Difficulties and Hazards. The *Camerons* behaved with their uſual Bravery, and *Lochiel* their chief was ſorely wounded in the Ankle. Being overpowered and obliged to retire before his Enemy, he was cloſely attended by his Brother the Doctor, who dreſſed, and took all imaginable Care of his Wound, till it was healed. The next Day, *Lochiel* marched with his Clan to the Side of a Hill, where he drew them up, and ordered the Pipes to play all the following Night, ſuch Tune as he knew, would beſt divert and amuſe them In their preſent melancholy Circumſtances. The next Morning, finding there was no Likelihood of his being joined by any conſiderable Force, and that there was no Subſiſtence for his Troops, marched away for *Lochabar*, along thoſe Hills that ſeparate that County from *Badenoch*, and in two Days came to *Glengary*, where he found his unhappy Maſter, whose Grief was renewed on the Sight of his Friend, *Lochiel,* and so many miserable Objects with him; *Lochiel* himself dangerously wounded in the Ankle, and hardly able to travel, and a great Part of his Men in no better, many of them in a much worse Condition, tho' Dr. *Cameron* did all in his Power to relieve them in their Misery. Nothing was heard among them but Lamentations for their Miscarriage, and their present Misery and Distress, Groans uttered from a Sense of their aking Wounds; and many ready to drop under the Weight of their own Bodies, thro' Fatigue and Want of Refreshment. This was a Heart-breaking Sight to the Chevalier, who was less able to bear the Misfortunes of others than he was his own.

BUT nothing could exceed the Love of the *Camerons* for their *Lochiel,* unless it was that of the *Macdonalds* for their *Keppoch* · For being wounded in the very Height and Fury of the Battle, two of them took hold of his Legs, a third supported his Head, while the Rest posted themselves round him as an impregnable Bulwark; and in that Manner carried him from the Field, over the small River *Nairn,* to a Place of Safety.

GLENGARY having refreshed his Guests with Butter, Cheese, Milk, and Usquebaugh (a favourite Liquor among the Highlanders) the Chevalier held a Council of War with his Officers, wherein it was moved, to set up a Standard near that Place, and issue out Orders for the dispersed Troops to repair to it. This Proposal was agreed to by some who thought it was the best Method they could take, to secure themselves from being taken by the Enemy, as they certainly would be, in Case they were to separate, or wander about in small Parties. The Chevalier, however, truely informed them, that he had no more Money to give them; and therefore, unless they were able to force the Royalists in their Camp, they would run the utmost Hazard of having their Subsistence cut off. *Sullivan* and *Sheridan* spoke on the same Side, and expatiated on the Madness and Folly of such a Project. However, to keep their Fidelity and Constancy to their Master unshaken, these two Gentlemen assured them, that, upon their certain Knowledge, there were large Supplies of Men and Money, at that Instant, coming to them from *France,* and expected every Day, which would undoubtedly give a very favourable Turn to their Master's Affairs.

AT length after much Debate, it was agreed, that the *Camerons* should keep in a Body, and march together to
Achnacary,

Achnacory, Lochiel's Seat, on the Road to *Fort-William,* and about nine Miles from it; where, by their patrolling Parties, they might obferve the Motions of the Royalifts; while the Chevalier, with the Corps under him, performed the fame Service upon the Quarter toward *Invernefs.*

PURSUANT to this Refolution, *Lochiel* with his *Camerons* marched away for *Achnacary;* and the firft Thing they did, on their Arrival there, was, to fecure their beft Effects in the Woods, and fubterraneous Caverns, of which there were many in that Part of the Country, and confidering how foon the Royalifts might deprive them of their Cattle, they killed and fed upon them in a very plentiful Manner.

IN the mean Time, feveral of the broken Corps and Straglers, that had hid themfelves from the Fury of the Enemy, fome half dead with their Wounds, and all near famifhed for Want of Nourifhment, were continually coming in, and gave difmal Accounts, tho' often at the Expence of Truth, of the Cruelty of the Royalifts For, I believe, it will be allowed, that never was lefs Barbarity fhewn on the like Occafion, as might be undeniably proved from Hiftory. The Chevalier was extremely affected at the piteous and lamentable Accounts they gave, and ufually faid, ' I am forry to have brought any fuch Hardfhips upon this ' poor People; and the beft Way to prevent the like for ' the Future, is to give over all further Attempts; for ' our Caufe is now defperate, and would to God I had ' died in the Field ! ' The Duke of *Perth,* however, and ' the other Noblemen, being willing to diffipate his Me- ' lancholy and relieve his Spirits, propofed a Hunting- ' Match: For, faid they, by this Means we may better ' efcape the Search of the Troops, if advancing towards us, ' or perhaps they may pafs by us, as Gentlemen only tak- ' ing their Diverfion.' This was agreed to, and they diverted themfelves in this Manner for fome Days, when they were informed of the March of General *Campbel,* with a large Body of the *Argylefhire* Militia from *Invernefs.* Upon which the Chevalier, with the Chiefs who were with him, *Sullivan* and *Sherridan,* and about forty others, marched away to *Achnacary,* where they found *Lochiel,* who was then under the Care of Dr. *Cameron* his Brother, for the Cure of his Wounds. *Lochiel* no fooner faw them, but prefently gueffing the Truth, haftily afked the Chevalier, what Body of the Royalifts it was that they had retired from? ' The *Campbels,* faid he, and added, And by this
Time,

' Time, I believe, they are at *Glengary*, for they set out
' Yesterday from *Invernefs*.' ' I thought so, answered
' *Lochiel*; for those Men would, surely, not be the last to
' the ruining of us, as they have done many other brave
' and loyal Clans.' The Chevalier, upon hearing this,
would have gone away directly, had not *Lochiel* assured
him, that the *Campbels* would be very careful to desolate
the Places through which they passed. ' Consider, said he,
' that *Stratherrick* and *Glengary* lie betwixt them and me,
' and these to be sure, they will sift e're they come to this
' Place.' He was so far right in his Conjecture, that tho'
they behaved civilly enough in the Places where they came,
yet they made a very strict Search all over *Stratherrick* for
Lord *Lovat*, who had left his Abode about two Hours after
the Chevalier had taken his Leave of him.

THE Chevalier being prevailed upon by *Lochiel's* Arguments, sat down to Table, which was plentifully spread
with Provisions of all Sorts, and Wine, and other Liquors
in Abundance, which the Highlanders get, at a very cheap
Rate, from *France*, for there being no Officers of Excise
in those Parts, except at *Fort-William*, where there is a
Garrison, prodigious Quantities of Liquors are run upon
that Coast, in Exchange for their Cattle, which they slaugh-
ter and barrel up for that Purpose:

LOCHIEL, however mistaken in his political Notions,
was, as hath been before observed, a Gentleman of strict
Honour, and inviolably attached to the Chevalier's Interest; with him, therefore, he consulted, what was best to
be done in this Emergency. Some advised to fight the
Campbels as soon as they came up, others disapproved that
Proposal, as it would farther enrage the Enemy, weaken
themselves and furnish the *Campbels* with Pretences to dispos-
sess them of their Goods and Chattels, which they would
enjoy as a Reward of their Service. After much Debate, it
was concluded to sculk about in a Body, till the promised
Succours from *France* arrived. ' But, said *Lochiel*, since
' the Enemy is so very near us, let us live as well as possible
' in the mean Time, lest those come to take up our Goods,
' who will give us little or no Thanks for them. Mean
' while my Clan may be driving their Cattle to the securest
' Places, and my Servants concealing my most valuable
' Effects.'

THE *Camerons* took his Advice, and drove their Cattle
into Places of the greatest Safety, and then went down
Morvain

Morvaiz, and drew themfelves into a Body, as by their Chief they were directed. In the mean Time his Servants buried his Plate, and beſt Furniture in the Çaves and Hollows that were about his Houſe, which being done, and the Enemy approaching, the whoſe Company left the Houſe, which was foon afterwards burnt down to the Ground.

SOME Time after, a Party of Brigadier *Houghton's* Regiment coming to *Acknacary*, and finding every Thing defolated and deſtroy'd, and Nobody to be feen, fearch'd for the Treaſure, which, they ſuppoſed, might be hid thereabouts; but, probably would have loſt their Labour, had they not ſpied the Gardener, who being anxious for the Safety of his Maſter's Effects, lurk'd about the Place. Him they fecured and examined, but on his pretending Ignorance, they tied him to two Halberts, and laſhed him on the naked Back with Rods, till the Smart forced him to diſcover the Place of Concealment, where they found the hidden Treaſure, and then diſmiſs'd the Man to his Maſter to acquaint him with what he had ſeen and ſuffered.

IN the mean Time, *Lochiel*, with the Chevalier and his Retinue, having left *Achnacary*, were come to the Green of *Keppoch*, and took up his Lodgings in that Chief's Houſe; where he was no fooner arriv'd, but his Ears were pierced with the Cries and Lamentations of a widow and ſix fatherleſs Children, for *Keppoch* was dead of the wounds he received at the Battle of *Culloden*, and his Clan were juſt return'd from the Funeral of their Maſter. This mournful Scene afflicted the Chevalier to the very Soul, and melted his whole Retinue into Tears. *Lochiel* however, and the two *Iriſh* Favourites, endeavour'd to argue him into a better Senfe of Things, and faid, it was below the Dignity of a Man, and unworthyof a Chriſtian, to indulge an Exceſs of Grief in the Day of Adverſity. and the Chevalier, recollecting his ſcatter'd Spirits, faid, ' We muſt ' act and not mourn; and I think it is proper, that theſe ' People (pointing to the *Macdonalds* of *Keppoch*) ſhould ' join with the *Camerons*, and keep in a Body, till an Opportunity offers, either of making Head againſt the Uſur-' per's Forces, or elſe getting over to *France*, where I ſhall ' be fure to get them incorporated with the *Scots* and *Iriſh* ' Regiments in the Pay of that Crown.' This Propoſal was approved; and after the whole Company had refreſh'd themſelves with a plentiful Dinner, the Servants of *Keppoch*

were

were ordered to carry away and ſecrete the moſt valuable
Effects in the Houſe, which they did ſo effectually, that
the Royaliſts could never find them, tho' the Houſe was
burnt to the Ground.

THE Chevalier and his Chiefs, in the mean while, held
a freſh Conſultation, in which they came to the following
Reſolution. ' That *Lochiel*, with the *Camerons* and *Macdonalds*, ſhould keep in a Body, and favour any Land-
' ings from *France*, while the Chevalier, with his Favou-
' rites, *Sullivan*, *Sheridan*, and others, were to traverſe
' the Iſle, and endeavour to raiſe ſuch a Force, as with
' the Succour from abroad, might enable him to make a
' Stand.' The next Morning they ſet out for *Glenphillin*,
where, at his firſt Landing, the *Camerons* erected his
Standard. Here they made a Cave the place of their Re-
ſidence, placed at proper Diſtances, for Six Miles round.
They were provided with every Thing for the Support of
Life; but the Chevalier being uneaſy in his Mind, after
three Days Abode there, ſet out for the Iſles.

IMMEDIATELY after the Battle of *Culloden*, the Duke
of *Cumberland* iſſued a Proclamation, promiſing Mercy to
thoſe who peaceably ſubſiſted, and threatening Vengeance
to thoſe that were refractory; which had ſuch an Effect,
that great Numbers laid down their Arms, and were
ſent quietly to their own Homes. So that by the 20th of
May, moſt of the Clans, together with many of their
Chiefs, had embraced the Duke's Terms; and ſcarce any
continued in Arms, except the *Camerons*, ſome of the
Macdonalds of *Keppoch*, and *John Roy Steuart*

Lochiel remained a conſiderable Time in the Cave, while
the Chevalier wandered up and down the Country, ſuffer-
ing many Evils, and in continual Danger of falling into
the Hands of his Enemies, yet ſtill looking out for ſome
French Ship that might carry him away. At length a ſmall
Schooner of about 18 or 20 Tons, arrived in the Harbour
of *Flota*, in the Iſle of *South Uiſt*, where the Chevalier, his
Friend *Lochiel*, and Dr. *Cameron* happen'd then to be. In
this Veſſel they joyfully embark'd, and the next Morning,
which was *September* 17, they ſet Sail for *Bologn*, where,
after a quick Paſſage, they ſafely arrived, to the Surprize
of their Friends, and their own great Satisfaction.

Lochiel had immediately a Regiment given him in the
French Army, and the Doctor was made Phyſician to the
ſame, and ſo continued to the Death of his Brother,
which

which happen'd in *September* 1748. After this, he was Phyfician to the Lord *Ogilvie*'s Regiment; now quartered at *Lifle*.

ABOUT three Years ago a Collection was made among thofe who were Friends to the Pretender's Caufe, for the Support of his unhappy Adherents Abroad. Dr. *Cameron* then came over to *England* to receive a Part of thofe Contributions. Another Collection has been fet on Foot for the fame Purpofe, and the Doctor made Inftances to his Friends here in *England*, for a Part in the fame ; reprefenting by his Letters that his Pay in the Army was not fufficient to fupport him and his numerous Family. But after many Sollicitations, not receiving any fatisfactory Anfwer, came over himfelf, and this was the Bufinefs that brought him to *Scotland*, when he was difcovered and brought to *London* The Manner of his Apprehenfion we are well affured was as follows .

ON *Monday March* 26, Dr. *Cameron*, Brother to *Lochiel*, who was engaged in the laft Rebellion, and attainted, was brought Prifoner to the Caftle of *Edinburgh* , he was taken by a Party of Lord *George Beauclerk*'s Regiment, who was detached from the Fort at *Inverfnaid* in Search of him ; this Detachment was commanded by one Capt *Graven :* They had Information of the Houfe where he was to ftay fome Days, but in their March to it, were obliged to pafs through two finall Villages , at the End of the firft they faw a little Girl, who, as foon as fhe perceived Soldiers, ran as faft as fhe could , a Serjeant and two or three Men purfued her, but fhe reached the other Village before they could overtake her , and there fhe fent off a Boy; who feemed to be placed there to give Intelligence of the Approach of the Soldiers. The Soldiers then purfued the Boy, but finding they were not able to come up with him, the Serjeant called out to his Men to prefent their Pieces, as if they intended to fhoot him The Boy on this, turning round, begg'd his Life , they fecured him, and then went to the Houfe where the Doctor was, which they befet on all Sides. The Difpofition the Captain made was admirable , he with fome of his Men marched up to the Front of the Houfe, but was foon difcovered from the Window, where he was immediately fecured by the Serjeant before-mentioned, who was placed there, as the Cap-

E   tain

tain very judiciously suspected the Doctor might attempt an Escape from that Part of the House

When he was brought to the Castle here, the Lord Justice *Clark*, went to him and told him, " You are the only Man in your Circumstances, that ever I had Occasion to speak to, (since I have been engaged in Business) whose Answer to me could be of no Prejudice to him   Because you are to be carried to *London*, and there are Witnesses ready to appear against you at the Court of King's Bench, to prove that you are the identical Doctor *Cameron* mentioned in the Bill of Attainder, this, Sir, will condemn you, and you are to have no further Trial, " This struck him, and after some Pause, he replied, " That he did not come over with a political Design, but only to transact some Affairs relating to *Lochiel's* Estate "

AMONG other Methods which the Parliament took to extinguish the Pretender's Hopes for the future, they made an Act to attaint several eminent Persons among the Rebels, in Case they did not surrender themselves to the Government by a Day appointed.   None of them, however, that were therein mentioned, came in or surrender'd, except Secretary *Murray*, who thought to merit the Favour of the Government by becoming Evidence against Lord *Lovat*. Dr. *Cameron* was unhappily in the same List, and consequently liable to the Penalty of the Statute whenever he should be taken in the Realms.

AFTER Dr *Cameron* had been some Time a Prisoner in *Edinburgh* Castle, he was conveyed to *London*, and after his Arrival, was examined before the Council at the *Cockpit*, where he disowned himself to be the identical Person mentioned in the Bill of Attainder, which obliged the Secretaries to look out for some of those Witnesses, who had given Evidence at the Trials of the Rebels in 1746

THURSDAY Morning, *May* 17, Dr. *Cameron* was carried from the Tower (attended by several of the Warders and a Party of the Guards) to the Court of King's-Bench, and there arraign'd upon the Act of Attainder passed against him and others, for being in the late Rebellion, and not surrendering in due Time. The four Judges were on the Bench, and the Prisoner not being desirous to give the Court any Trouble, readily acknowledged himself to be the identical Person; whereupon, after due Deliberation, **the** Lord Chief Justice *Lee* pronounced the following moving

ing Sentence; ' You *Archibald Cameron* of *Lochiel*, in that
' Part of *Great Britain* called *Scotland*, muft be removed
' from hence to his Majefty's Prifon of the Tower of *Lon-*
' *din*, from whence you came, and on *Thurfday* the 7th of
' *June* next your Body to be drawn on a Sledge to the
' Place of Execution, there to be hanged, not till you are
' dead; your Bowels to be taken out, your Body quar-
' tered, and your Head cut off, and affixed at the King's
' Difpofal, and the Lord have Mercy on your Soul.' On
receiving the Sentence, he made a genteel Bow, and only
defired he might have Leave to fend for his Wife, who
with feven Children, entirely dependant on him for Support, are now at *Lifle* in *Flanders*, which was granted. He
faid, that in 1746, he came from *France* to furrender himfelf, agreeable to the Proclamation, but was prevented by
an Accident happening in his Family. He behaved with
great Refolution before the Court, and anfwered to every
Queftion with a becoming Decency.

DURING the Interval between the Sentence and his Execution, his Wife ufed all poffible Means to obtain a Pardon,
by delivering a Petition to his Majefty, another to her Royal
Highnefs the Princefs of Wales, and to feveral of the No-
bility , but without Effect. For on *Thurfday*, *June* 7th he
was conveyed in a Hurdle from the Tower, to *Tyburn*, and
there executed agreeable to his Sentence. His Behaviour
was all along firm and intrepid, yet decent and folid, and
becoming a Man who expected, yet feared not, the Stroke
of Death.

ON *Wednefday*, Orders were fent to the Tower that the
Gates fhould be fhut at Six o'Clock in the Evening, and
no Perfons whatever admitted thro' after that Hour, to prevent any Attempts that might be made to favour his Efcape.

As foon as his Wife arrived from *Flanders*, fhe immediately repaired to her Hufband in the Tower, who received
her with all that Tendernefs and Affection, which the
Greatnefs and Solemnity of the Occafion could infpire.
The Grief and Anguifh of her Soul is much more eafily
imagined than defcribed. She came to take her laft Fare-
wel of him, who, by all the Ties of mutual Affection,
was dearer to her than all the World And as an Aggra-
vation to her Affliction, fhe not only faw herfelf about to be
deprived of an affectionate Hufband, but to be left deftitute

of

of a Support for herſelf, and her numerous Family. Their Children, the dear Pledges of their Loves, muſt now be expoſed to all the Neceſſities and Caſualties of Life, without the Patronage of a kind and indulgent Father to have recourſe to for Advice and Aſſiſtance. The Conſideration of this Train of Evils, now haſtening upon her, made ſuch a ſtrong Impreſſion on her Mind, as to force a Flood of Tears from her mournful Eyes. The Doctor comforted her as well as he could, and deſired her to uſe all the Means in her Power to ſave his Life, which was to preſent a Petition in his Favour to his Majeſty, who, perhaps, might be prevailed upon to ſave him.

In the Morning of his Execution, ſhe took her laſt Leave of him, indeed it was a very mournful one, and melted thoſe who ſaw it into Tears. The Exceſs of her Grief has ſo affected her Senſes, that ſhe is now diſtracted; ſo great was her Love for her Huſband, and ſo intenſe her Sorrow for his ſad Cataſtrophe.

As ſoon as ſhe was gone, the Doctor put himſelf in a Readineſs to receive the Sheriff and thoſe who were ſent to conduct him to his Execution. Accordingly, about Ten o'Clock he was brought out of the *Tower*, by a Party of the Horſe Guards who delivered him to the Sheriffs of *London* and *Middleſex* as ſoon as he was come without the *Tower-Gate*. He was then put into the Hurdle, to which he was faſtened by the Executioner. In this Manner he was drawn thro' the City, attended by Sir *Richard Glynn*, one of the Sheriffs, and under the Care of the Sheriff's-Officers and Conſtables, to the Place of Execution. Sir *Charles Aſgill*, left the Priſoner at the *Tower*, and Sir *Richard Glynn* followed the Sledge from the *Tower*, in his Chariot, to *Tyburn*.

The Doctor was dreſſed in a light coloured Coat, red Waiſtcoat and Breeches, and new Bag-wig. In his Paſſage thro' the Streets, he was obſerved to look about, as if in Admiration of the vaſt Multitude of Spectators that crouded the Streets, Windows, and Balconies to ſee him paſs, and bowed to ſeveral Perſons, about Twelve o'Clock he arrived at the Place of Execution.

Being arrived at the Place of Execution, and helped into the Cart, he deſired to ſpeak with the Sheriff; who being come to him, the Doctor entreated the Favour of him, that he would give Orders to his Officers to let his Body hang till he was quite dead, before the Executioner

begun

begun his further Operation. The Sheriff promifed to oblige him in his Requeft, and accordingly the Body was permitted to hang full three Quarters of an Hour, and was not cut down before it was very certain, that no Life was remaining in him.

He had likewife fome Difcourfe with the Executioner about the Difpofal of his Body after Execution was performed, which he defired might be decently put in a Coffin, and conveyed to Mr. *Stephenfon's* the Undertaker, and that his Cloaths might be given to his Friends, in lieu of which, that he might not lofe his ufual Perquifite, he bid him take what Money was in his Pockets.

While he was in the Cart, a Gentleman, in a Lay-Habit, came to him, and pray'd with him for about a Quarter of an Hour, and then left him to his private Devotions. From this Incident, the Spectators imagined that the Doctor was a *Roman Catholick*, and that the Gentleman who pray'd with him, was a Prieft

But whatever his Religion was, he died with great Steadinefs, Conftancy, and Refolution, without any vifible Alteration in his Countenance or Behaviour, but perfectly refign'd to the Will of Heaven, and chearfully acquiefcing with the Sentence which the Laws of his Country had paffed upon him.

He made no publick Profeffion of his Faith, nor declared what Religion he was of; nor did he addrefs the People in a Speech; nor did he give any Letters or Papers to the Sheriff, or any other Gentleman prefent at the Execution: So that if any Thing of this Kind fhould hereafter be publifh'd, we may look upon it as fpurious.

His Body being taken down from the Gallows, the Executioner cut off the Head, and took out the Bowels, but did not quarter the Body. His Body and Head were put into a Coffin, with this Infcription upon it, Dr. *Archibald Cameron*, Suffer'd the 7th of *June*, 1753, Aged 46. A Hearfe convey'd it to Mr. *Stephenfon's* Undertaker, oppofite *Exeter Change*.

F I N I S.

Juſt Publiſh'd,

I. **A** Charge to the Clergy of the Dioceſe of *London*, Occaſioned by a general Viſitation held at St. *Paul's* on *Thurſday*, May 17, 1753. Price 6 d.

II. An Apology for the Naturalization of the Jews, Price 6 d.

III. The Falſe Accuſers: or who drank the P——'s Health? A Sermon lately preach'd in a Chaple near St. James's. Price 6 d.

IV. Royal Folly: or David's Sin in numbering of the People: A Sermon preach'd at St Mary's in Oxford, on Sunday, April 1. occaſioned by a Deſign on Foot of regiſtring the People of Great Britain. Price 6 d.

V. Memoirs of the Life of Robert Devereux, Earl of Eſſex, being a full Explanation of all the Paſſages in the New Tragedy of the Earl of Eſſex. Price 1 s.

Printed for M. Cooper, Pater-noſter-row, W. Reeve, Fleet-ſtreet; and C. Sympſon, Chancery-lane.

Lightning Source UK Ltd.
Milton Keynes UK
UKHW020936280620
365582UK00003B/165